106 Claudia

Claudia

796.93   Washington,
Wa   Rosemary G
c.1   Cross-country
          skiing is for me

DATE DUE

Claudia

CROSS-COUNTRY
SKIING is for me

CROSS-COUNTRY SKIING is for me

Rosemary G. Washington

photographs by
Robert L. Wolfe

Lerner Publications Company   Minneapolis

The author wishes to thank Paul Martin of Midwest Moun-
taineering Outdoor Equipment and Clothing, Lois and Ruth
Austerman, David Merfeld, Bert Schmitt, Jr., Mark Lerner,
and Laura Storms for their assistance with this book.

Photographs on pages 38 and 39 courtesy of the American
Birkebeiner. Photographs on pages 40 and 41 courtesy of
the Canadian Ski Marathon.

LIBRARY OF CONGRESS CATALOGING IN PUBLICATION DATA

Washington, Rosemary G.
 Cross-country skiing is for me.

 (A Sports for me book)
 Summary: Lois and her friend describe cross-country
skiing, including appropriate dress, equipment,
ski waxing techniques, and such basic moves as the
diagonal stride, step turn, herringbone, and snowplow.
  1. Cross-country skiing — Juvenile literature.
[1. Cross-country skiing. 2. Skis and skiing]
I. Wolfe, Robert L., ill. II. Title.
III. Series: Sports for me books.
GV855.3.W37   796.93   82-7225
ISBN 0-8225-1126-6   AACR2

Manufactured in the United States of America

International Standard Book Number: 0-8225-1126-6
Library of Congress Catalog Card Number: 82-7225

2 3 4 5 6 7 8 9 10 91 90 89 88 87 86 85 84 83

Hi! My name is Lois. I just got a letter from my penpal. Her name is Katarina, and she lives in Norway. Cross-country skiing, my favorite sport, began in Norway hundreds of years ago.

Cross-country skiing is skiing across the countryside. Parks, golf courses, or forest trails are good places to cross-country ski. You can ski uphill, downhill, or on flat ground. You need about three inches of snow cover for good skiing, but six inches is even better.

I learned to ski last winter, but it didn't snow very much. This year we've had lots of snow, so I've been practicing hard. Even when I'm not skiing, I try to keep my body in shape. When I'm in shape, I don't tire so quickly when I ski. It's easy to catch cold if you're tired.

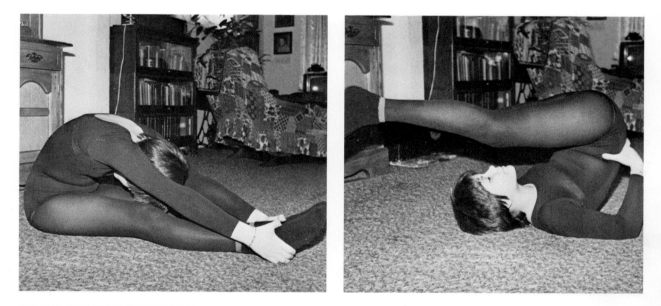

I can stay in shape in the summer, or off season, by running and bicycling. These exercises are good for my legs. During the ski season, I do stretching exercises every day. Stretching helps prevent pulled muscles and other injuries. These are some of the stretching exercises I do.

7

This year I got skis of my very own. My mom took me to a good ski shop to buy them. It's important to buy your equipment from salespeople who ski cross country themselves. They can fit you correctly and give you advice about skiing, too.

Cross-country skis are longer and narrower than downhill skis. I got **touring skis**, which are good all-purpose skis.

Cross-country skiers who race often buy **racing skis**. Racing skis are very light and are narrower than touring skis.

Your skis must be the right size for you. To find your correct ski length, raise an arm above your head. The tip of the ski should reach your wrist.

When choosing skis, it is important to check the skis' **camber**. Camber is the slight arch in the middle of the ski. Camber gives the skis the ability to grip the snow and glide smoothly over it. The camber is correct when a piece of paper can be slipped under the ski while you stand on it. You should also be able to flatten the ski when standing on it with both feet.

My mom said I could get new ski boots, too. The man at the store was careful about fitting me properly. The boots should fit you comfortably. I always wear mine with two pairs of wool socks.

Boots can be waterproofed to prevent your feet from getting wet and cold. Or some people like to wear **gaiters**. Gaiters are pieces of material that tie around your ankles. They keep loose powder snow from melting inside your boots.

Bindings hold the boots to the skis. Cross-country ski bindings are **toe bindings**. The toe is pinned or clamped to the ski, and the heel is free. A **heel plate** helps to keep your heels from sliding off the sides of the skis.

13

The only other ski equipment you need are **poles**. You need poles to help you keep your balance and move over the snow. Poles are made of Tonkin bamboo, fiberglass, or metal. The salesperson helped me find poles that were the right length for me. They should be long enough to fit under your armpits.

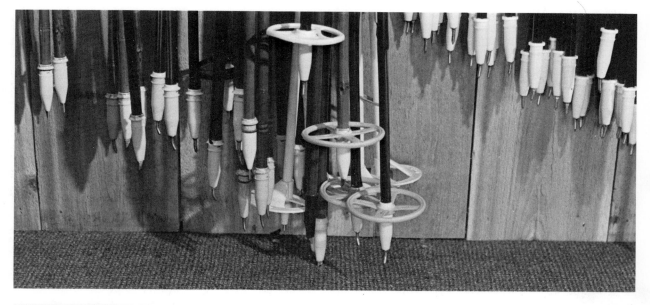

At the end of each pole is a **basket**. The baskets make it easier to push off in deep snow. The very tip of each pole is curved forward and pulls out of the snow easily.

You don't need any special clothes for cross-country skiing. But it is important to dress properly and comfortably. Even when you're out on a very cold day, you'll keep warm from the exercise. For that reason, you should wear several layers of light clothing.

As you get warmer, you can remove a layer or two until you're more comfortable. Wool is especially good. It absorbs moisture in case you start to sweat and keeps you from getting chilled from wet clothes.

Knickers, or short pants, are helpful but not necessary. Be sure to wear a warm hat and gloves or mittens, too.

I was really anxious to try out my new equipment. Was I ever happy when I looked out the window and saw that it had snowed during the night! The ground was covered with snow, and I could hardly wait to go skiing.

After breakfast I called my friend Dave
and asked him if he wanted to go skiing
with me. My neighbor, Bert, drove us to
the park. Bert is an older friend who had
helped Dave and me learn how to ski.

There were already ski tracks in the snow
when we got to the park. We weren't the
only people with skiing on our minds!

Before we started skiing, though, we had to get our skis ready. Some skis, such as most wooden ones and some fiberglass ones, have to be **waxed** before you can ski. The wax grips the snow and prevents you from slipping.

I use special waxes for different snow conditions. Hard waxes work in cold, dry snow. For mushy or warmer snow, I rub on soft waxes. Really sticky waxes called **klisters** come in tubes. Katarina had told me that *klister* means "glue" in Norwegian.

To smooth the wax onto the ski, buff the bottoms of the skis quickly and lightly with a cork. The friction caused by rubbing warms the wax so it smoothes on evenly.

Dave's skis are **no-wax**, so his were ready to go. Fiberglass skis like his have special raised patterns on the bottoms. Some common patterns are the step, the fishscale, and the diamond. These patterns grip the snow much like wax does on waxable skis.

After Bert and I had waxed our skis, we were all ready to start skiing. We started out on flat ground. It was easier to ski on the tracks where the snow was packed than it was to ski on untracked snow. We did the **diagonal stride,** which is the most basic cross-country skiing movement.

To do the diagonal stride, you glide on one ski at a time. A **kick,** which is like pushing off from a skateboard, moves you forward. During the kick, your weight shifts over one ski. You press down and back on the weighted ski. This action pushes you forward.

For practice, Bert suggested I try the
diagonal stride without my poles. You
automatically shift your weight correctly
when you do the diagonal stride without
them. Let your arms swing and your heels
come up off the skis. Try to get a long glide
between kicks. Remember to look ahead
and not down at your skis. As you pick up
speed, press your upper body forward.

Bert said I was really getting the feel of the striding motion. So I decided to start using my poles again. Planting your poles after you swing your arms forward gives you additional forward motion. The diagonal stride is a lot like walking. You naturally move your right ski with your left pole and your left ski with your right pole.

Dave, Bert, and I were really enjoying ourselves. It was a very cold day, but the exercise kept us warm.

Soon we came to a small hill. Cross-country skiers can go uphill without sliding backward. You can do this because of the wax or pattern on your skis. To ski uphill, just shorten your strides and your poling.

On steeper hills you may have to use other uphill methods. One slow but sure method of getting up steep hills is the **side step.** To do the side step, stand sideways to the hill with your skis together. Move the top ski up the hill a little ways. Shift your weight to that ski. Then pick up the other ski and bring it alongside the first ski. Repeat these steps all the way up the hill.

You may also do the **herringbone**. This step leaves tracks in the snow that look like fish bones. Keep your poles behind your skis as you herringbone uphill. Put the tails of your skis together to form a *V.* Grip the hill with the inside edges of your skis.

Traversing the hill is another method of getting up a steep incline. To traverse the hill, you zigzag up the hill instead of going straight up. This makes the climb seem less steep.

There are special ways to ski downhill slowly and safely. One of these methods is the **snowplow.** To do the snowplow, we held the tips of our skis together and fanned out the tails, forming a *V.* This position prevented us from going down the hill too fast. To stop, just put more weight on the inside edges of your skis.

Most experienced skiers keep their skis parallel, or side by side, as they go downhill. Bert liked to ski downhill in the **telemark** position. To do this, he put one ski ahead of the other. His front leg dropped in a deep bend at the knee, and his trailing leg was extended straight back. His heel was raised a few inches off the trailing ski.

You need to know how to turn on skis so that you can avoid running into trees, bushes, or other skiers. Skiers can turn from the snowplow position. While holding your skis in the *V* shape, you simply shift your weight over one ski. If you want to turn to the left, you shift your weight over the right ski. To turn right, you do the opposite.

On a flat area or on a gentle slope, you can change direction with a **step turn.** Just pick up one ski and then step off at an angle. Your next motion will bring the other ski in the new direction.

You can do the step turn from a standing position, too. You pick up one ski and set it down at an angle. Then bring the other ski beside it. Continue to make small steps like these until you are pointed in the direction you want to go. You'll leave a very pretty star-like pattern in the snow.

To turn in one giant step instead of many smaller steps, use the **kick turn**. Begin with both skis side by side. Plant your poles apart and out of the way to the outside edge of one ski. Using the poles for balance, pick up the tip of the other ski and swing it completely around. Set it beside the first ski, tips to tails.

Next swing your back pole around in the same direction that you moved your ski. At this point, both poles and one ski will be set in the new direction. Finally you lift the other ski and bring it beside the first.

By this time Dave and I were getting a little tired, so we headed for the warming house for some hot chocolate. Dave began **double-poling** to pick up speed. Double-poling is working your arms together so that you plant both poles at the same time.

Dave bent at the waist and knees and then shifted his body weight down between the poles. As he glided by the poles, he straightened his arms to get extra forward push. You can also use double-poling with leg kicks.

We felt great after all that exercise in the snow. We really didn't get too cold because we were always moving. It was nice to stop and rest indoors, though. We sipped hot chocolate and talked about skiing. As we relaxed, Bert told us about a race that was coming up soon.

Skiers often test their skiing skills in races. Some of the longer races, like the American Birkebeiner, are **marathons**. Marathons are long-distance races. Katarina told me that *birkebeiner* means "birch legs" in Norwegian. What a funny name for skis!

The American Birkebeiner is over 30 miles long. Even the fastest skiers take over three hours to finish this race.

The Canadian Ski Marathon is even longer. This race is 100 miles long and lasts two days. Hundreds of people compete in these long races. To begin, all the racers line up side by side for a **massed start.**

People like me who ski just for fun have many chances to race, too. Races are often held at the park where I ski. Even beginners can participate. Children and adults start the race together. But winners are chosen from several age groups, or **classes.** I race in the junior class.

Dave and I decided to enter the race at the park. The course followed a trail through the park and along a frozen lake. There were two hills on the course, so I knew I'd have to use many of the skills I had been practicing.

I got off to a good start. I tried to ski smoothly, matching my arm swings with my leg strides. I rode the glides with my feet flat on the gliding ski. I stayed on the prepared tracks. When I was ready to pass another skier, I called out, "Track!" The slower skier stepped aside, and I moved ahead.

The hills were too steep to use the diagonal stride, so I used the herringbone instead. I bounded from ski to ski, trying not to lose any speed. The finish line was not far from the bottom of the second hill. I double-poled across as fast as I could.

I finished third in my class! Dave did well, too. Everyone who finished the race won a T-shirt. I think I'll send mine to Katarina when I write and tell her about the race. Some day I'd like to visit Katarina in Norway and go skiing with her. Cross-country skiing is for me!

Words about CROSS-COUNTRY SKIING

BIATHLON: An Olympic event that combines cross-country skiing with rifle shooting skills

BINDER: A glue-like substance that holds wax on skis

BINDINGS: The toe clamps that hold the boots onto the skis

CLASS: A group of skiers in the same age and/or sex group

DIAGONAL STRIDE: The basic kick and glide motion of cross-country skiing

DOUBLE-POLING: A method of picking up speed by increasing forward thrust off poles that are both planted at the same time

GAITERS: Leggings that cover the top of a ski boot, preventing snow from getting inside

HEEL PLATE: A device on the ski that prevents the heel from sliding off the side of the ski

HERRINGBONE: A method of climbing uphill with your ski tips spread widely apart

KICK: The push-off that provides forward motion

KLISTER: Very sticky liquid wax used in snow that is slushy or icy

MARATHON: A long-distance race

PARALLEL: A method of skiing downhill with your skis held close together

SNOWPLOW: A method of skiing downhill at controlled speeds. The ski tips are held closely together and the tails are spread widely apart.

TELEMARK: A downhill ski position in which one ski is held in front of the other and the skier's front leg is bent

TRAVERSE: To zigzag back and forth across a hill

ABOUT THE AUTHOR

ROSEMARY G. WASHINGTON, an avid cross-country skier, is a freelance writer and graphic designer living in Seattle, Washington. She graduated from the University of Minnesota and has been a staff editor and book designer for a juvenile book publisher.

ABOUT THE PHOTOGRAPHER

ROBERT L. WOLFE studied photography at the Minneapolis College of Art and Design. For several years, he was a medical photographer at the University of Minnesota, where he also taught medical photography. Mr. Wolfe lives in Minneapolis with his wife and two children. His photos have appeared in several *Sports for Me* books.